TILBURY FORT

ESSEX

Paul Pattison

Tilbury Fort is one of the finest surviving 17th-century forts in England, occupying a strong defensive position on the Thames estuary, backed by open marshland. The present fort was begun in 1670, in the reign of Charles II, on the site of an earlier fort built by Henry VIII between 1539 and 1540. In West Tilbury nearby, Elizabeth I famously rallied her makeshift army awaiting the Armada in 1588.

In the 17th century, the fort's artillery was designed to stop warships on the river, and its garrison equipped to prevent land attack. Two magazines built in 1716 stored vast quantities of government gunpowder, destined for the fighting forces of the emerging Empire. After the failed Jacobite rebellion of 1745, Scots prisoners were briefly confined at Tilbury and are commemorated here. Long years of quiet garrison were succeeded by modernisation; gigantic rifled guns were added in the 1870s, and in 1902 new artillery was introduced to fight the emerging faster warships. During the First World War, the fort accommodated and supplied troops destined for the trenches, and the site became an important supply base for field army equipment.

Tilbury remained in military hands until 1950, when it was taken into care as a historic monument under the Ministry of Works.

❖ CONTENTS ❖

Tilbury Fort, No. 2 Office Block, The Fort, Tilbury, Essex RM18 7NR. Tel: 01375 858489

Published by English Heritage, 1 Waterhouse Square, 138-142 Holborn, London EC1N 2ST

First published by English Heritage 2004
Reprinted 2008, 2009, 2015, 2017
Revised reprint 2011, 2013, 2014

Commissioned by Susannah Lawson. Edited and designed by Patricia Briggs. Photography by Steve Cole.
Printed in England by Park Communications Ltd
C35, 04/17, 05355, *ISBN 978-1-85074-866-3*

Visit our website at
www.english-heritage.org.uk

TOUR OF THE FORT

The plans of the fort on p. 32 and the inside back cover should help you to find your way round. The ticket office is housed in what was the guard house.

Guard House

Tilbury Fort had an armed guard – usually twelve men commanded by a sergeant – on duty twenty-four hours a day. Each man took his turn as sentry on gate duty in full dress, checking all comings and goings, ensuring soldiers were properly dressed and had authority for their journey.

Although sentries performed their duty generally as required, some might surreptitiously admit persons not on official business, for example women wishing to see their men. (Before the late 19th century, very few soldiers were permitted to marry.) In the door to the side of the short entrance passage there is a spy-hole, through which can be seen a cell. This is where soldiers would have been confined following breaches of military discipline; drunkenness was particularly common and the cell was rarely empty.

In the main room of the guard house, a fire was maintained in the huge fireplace, by which sentries could warm up and dry out after duty in bad weather. A heavy curtain across the doorway would keep in the warmth; you can see the row of hooks designed

The Water Gate (left), and guard house and chapel (right), seen from the parade ground

to support a curtain pole. In a corner of the room is a rack holding six smooth-bore muskets, made in 1864, ready for emergency use by the guard.

At the far end of the guard house is a private room and office, used by the sergeant or a junior officer. Over time, this room served many purposes. In 1908, for example, it was in use as a store for bread and meat. The fine cast-iron fireplace bears the initials of Queen Victoria (VR), and also of the Board of Ordnance (BO), which was the government body that provided weapons and supplies to the Army until 1855, when it was succeeded by the War Office.

A fine Victorian cast-iron fireplace, in the guard house

Leave through the door, and go up the iron staircase. Turn left at the top to enter the chapel. (If it is locked, a key may be obtained from the ticket office.)

The chapel interior, showing the cross motif built into its windows

Chapel

Situated directly over the guard house, the chapel is one of the oldest surviving chapels built as part of a British artillery fortress. There is a small vestry, with another fine Board of Ordnance fireplace, and, beyond this, the chapel itself. Although the interior is now plain, the garrison would have kept its regimental colours proudly on display here. (The pews were brought from West Tilbury church in recent times.)

Throughout its life, the chapel was often used for other purposes, possibly because a chaplain was not always available, and also because it was not consecrated and therefore did not provide all services for births, marriages and deaths. These services were held at the nearby parish churches of West Tilbury and Chadwell St Mary; the registers of these churches have frequent entries from the fort's soldiers.

On leaving the chapel, bear slightly left to go along the infantry firing trench.

Looking across the river from here, you can appreciate how well the fort guarded the Thames. Below, you can see the low zig-zag brick wall of the west gun line, which directly overlooked the river before the addition of the modern concrete wall behind it. Each 'V' in the line was occupied by a cannon mounted on a

wooden carriage. The small rectangular brick building to the right is an expense magazine, where gunpowder was stored ready for use. Together with a corresponding east gun line, these defences formed the main battery of guns protecting the river channel until the 1870s.

Return to the iron staircase, pausing to look at the parade ground below.

Parade Ground

Although not all of the fort's buildings survive, enough remain to show their grouping around the parade ground, where the troops were drilled, trained, inspected, exercised and, sometimes, punished. The fort plan on the inside back cover will help you identify the officers' quarters, the general artillery store, the foundations of the soldiers' barracks, the gunpowder magazines and the Landport Gate.

For much of the 19th century the parade ground was grassed, although there was paving around the principal buildings. The erection of four large store buildings in the 1880s, and the movement of heavy equipment within the fort, notably during the First World War, demanded that further paving be laid. The present surface was completed in the 1970s.

A view from the west across the parade ground, with the gunpowder magazines on the left, the officers' quarters on the far side and the foundations of the soldiers' barracks in the foreground. The area on the right of the foundations was the site of a ball court

The soldiers' quarters c.1950 during demolition. In the foreground, the ball court has already gone but the barracks remain standing. To the right, on the parade ground, is one of the large mobilisation stores of the 1880s, later also demolished

Soldiers' Barracks

The foundations clearly visible on the parade ground below are those of the two-storey barracks, where the ordinary soldiers lived. These would have looked similar to the officers' quarters that can be seen on the opposite side of the parade ground.

The barracks were divided into small square rooms. Each contained a fireplace and was simply furnished with a table and benches, a cupboard and two beds. Originally, four men lived in each room and slept two to a bed, although sergeants enjoyed a room each. The larger open area at the end is a ball court, added in the 19th century, where the soldiers played 'fives' (a game similar to squash).

Cannon in their embrasures in the west bastion, showing how they protected the fort walls, moats and adjacent north-west bastion from attack

Go down the iron staircase and along the foot of the rampart, keeping to the left of the soldiers' barracks, towards the north-west bastion.

Ramparts and Bastions

Tilbury Fort is defined by an earth rampart faced by a brick curtain wall. The wall forms a parapet, protecting soldiers and artillery on the flat surface of the rampart. The openings in the wall, called embrasures, were for the artillery to fire through.

THE LIVES OF ❖ TILBURY'S SOLDIERS ❖

Between the 1680s and 1920s, Tilbury's garrison numbered between 100 and 300 soldiers, mostly regular infantry and artillery. Life was a mixture of routine and boredom. Repetitive guard duties, artillery drill, marching and training exercises ensured the men maintained the discipline essential for a close unit in the smoke and confusion of battle. But discipline was more relaxed in garrison than on campaign, and boredom could lead to gambling, brawling and drunkenness. The punishment for unruly behaviour could be severe, with soldiers being flogged or locked in the guard house cell.

In the 19th century, Tilbury was fortunate enough to have a separate canteen, a ball court and vegetable gardens just outside the fort wall. But facilities were otherwise primitive: barracks were tightly packed, with two men to every bed. Sanitation, where it existed, was in the form of a communal toilet – called the bog house – and a cold wash under the pumps on the parade ground. Barrack rooms could be quite unpleasant places, with an atmosphere thick with the smell of food, pipe and coal smoke, candle wax, damp clothes, body odour, dirty feet and the wooden tub that served as a night urinal.

Bad conditions in garrisons nationwide resulted in an Army Sanitary Commission in 1857, leading to gradual improvement. After 1880, better facilities were common. At Tilbury, these included married quarters, proper toilets, running water and washrooms, and a recreation and reading room. And for religious soldiers, there was a chapel.

Artillerymen of the fort garrison outside the Water Gate, May 1897

In plan, the fort has five equal sides and was designed to have a bastion projecting like an arrowhead at each corner, although only four bastions were completed. Each bastion has four faces, carefully angled so that the defending artillery and infantry not only had a clear view of the approaches to the fort, including the outer defences, but also a clear view across to adjacent bastions. This precise geometry

THE BASTION SYSTEM ❖ OF FORTIFICATION ❖

A bastion is a projecting part of a fortification built at an angle to the line of a wall, so as to allow defensive fire in several directions. The system ensures there are no gaps along the defences where an enemy could gain shelter from flanking fire (that is, fire directed along the face of the wall). An attack directed at one bastion can be repulsed by fire from others, and vice-versa.

Bastions developed from the towers on medieval fortifications and were first used regularly in Italy in the early 16th century. Along with the walls they protected, the bastions were lower and thicker than the earlier towers, presenting a more difficult and more robust target. The system developed to become very elaborate, with multiple lines and tiers of ramparts and bastions, carefully engineered to bring massive firepower to bear on an attacking force.

To keep an enemy at an even greater distance, further defences were devised – called outworks. Those at Tilbury are complex and impressive: multiple broad wet moats, incorporating ramparts and other defensive positions in and between them, ensured that an enemy attack would be slow, difficult and costly.

Aerial view of Tilbury Fort, clearly showing its impressive bastions and extensive outer defences

ensured that defensive fire could be targeted at the ground outside from several directions.

Go to the point of the north-west bastion.

Originally all four bastions would have looked like this one, although the interior here has been partially infilled, burying a ramp from the parade ground. It is possible to detect the grass-grown foundations of the married quarters, built here around 1900. Looking through one of the embrasures, you can see how the cannon protected the curtain wall and the adjacent bastions. From here you can also see the inner moat, part of the fort's elaborate outer defences.

A cannon stood behind each embrasure, and against the parapet were lockers holding a small, ready supply of gunpowder and shot. The English-made cannon here – an 18-pounder of around 1780–1810 – saw service at Tilbury. The circular concrete drum supported a spigot mortar during the Second World War.

Continue around the rampart to the Landport Gate (the building with the pitched roof). Stop on the concrete pad.

You are now standing over the passage of the Landport Gate, which served as the entrance to the fort from a road across the marshes. The room over the gate passage was traditionally known as the Dead House, because it was used as a temporary mortuary at one time, although for most of its life it provided accommodation and storage.

OUTER DEFENCES

The outer defences that can be seen from here are the best surviving example of their kind in Britain. There are two concentric moats separated by a strip of land that contains a low outer rampart (its grassy bank is just visible). The moats are filled from the River Thames. The earth rampart was shaped into angled faces, echoing those of the bastions themselves and providing a defensive position for infantry to direct overlapping fields of fire at an enemy trying to cross the outer moat. Soldiers could assemble at strategic points called 'places of arms' before moving safely behind the earth rampart along a track called the

The walled passage between the gunpowder magazines, looking towards the Landport Gate and the Dead House. The rails were installed in the First World War to take heavy supply waggons

The ravelin and the inner moat, with the outer bridge (centre right), viewed from the east

The inner bridge crosses the inner moat from the ravelin to the Landport Gate. The drawbridges are clearly visible

'covered way', in order to reinforce any point being attacked.

The approach to the Landport Gate was carefully designed to guard against an enemy assault. Immediately beneath you, a long wooden bridge crosses the inner moat to a small triangular island, called a ravelin. The current bridge is an exact replica of the original, complete with two drawbridges that could be lifted to prevent access. The ravelin was enclosed by its own rampart and gates and formed a strongpoint defending the bridges. A second bridge – also incorporating a lifting section – leads from the ravelin onto the covered way beyond. Finally, a narrow causeway leads from the covered way onto another triangular island, called a redan, in the outer moat. The redan incorporated a two-storey triangular tower, called a redoubt – an outer strongpoint from which troops could defend the approach road.

One of the Victorian iron water pumps on the parade ground

Retrace your steps and go out onto the parade ground, stopping at the nearest iron pump.

Water Pump

Tilbury Fort is situated on a marshland site near to a tidal river, so, before the arrival of piped water in 1877, fresh water was scarce. The garrison coped by channelling rainwater from the roofs of buildings into underground storage cisterns, and by drawing water up from below ground. This Victorian pump stands over the main well, 178 m (584.5 ft) deep, and over one of four cisterns under the parade ground.

Turn to look at the two large gunpowder magazines.

Gunpowder Magazines

These two large magazines, which held vast quantities of gunpowder to supply the army at large, are the only ones of the early 18th century in Britain. Originally both had high-pitched roofs, but these were reduced in the 19th century to make the magazines less visible from a distance. The 18th-century blast wall around the magazines was built partly for security but mainly to provide some protection for the garrison in the event of an explosion; gunpowder is volatile and a single spark could be catastrophic.

Go through the doorway marked 'east gunpowder magazine'.

The east magazine is a strong building, with thick walls and heavy buttresses designed to contain an accidental explosion. Nevertheless, the walls comprise decorative orange and yellow brickwork on this side (although the other sides are plain) and the lead drainpipes and heads were painted. The mark 'GR 1719' can be seen on the nearest one, commemorating its completion in the reign of George I. The door is faced in copper, which would not spark.

Inside, further measures are apparent to minimise the risk of a spark. There is no iron anywhere and the floorboards are secured to joists with wooden pegs. The floor is raised on brick arches, while the walls have vertical slots to keep the building cool and dry so that the gunpowder would not become damp and spoil. The windows are 19th-century alterations.

In 1730–1, twin vaults replaced an original single large vault. The internal walls were once lined with wood. The magazine would have been stacked to within 60 cm (2 ft) of the roof, with rows of large barrels held on timber racking, leaving corridors

One of the lead rainwater heads on the east gunpowder magazine; note the painted initials 'GR' for King George I

The heavy buttresses of the east gunpowder magazine

Detail of the copper sheeting, with its decorative nails, over the door to the east gunpowder magazine

for access and shifting. The racking is a reconstruction of the original. This magazine could accommodate 4500 barrels, each holding 45 kg (100 lbs); those on display are exact replicas.

There is an exhibition about the fort's history in this magazine.

Leave the magazine, go back through the blast wall and turn left, heading between the magazine and the terrace of houses.

North-East Bastion

The structures here date from between 1868 and 1871, when new emplacements for artillery were installed on the rampart, and dedicated magazines, shell stores and cartridge stores were built underground.

Go to the second pair of doorways and in through the right-hand entrance.

The passage contains part of a wooden barrier marking the place where a soldier changed into special clothing and shoes made of materials that minimised the risk of sparking an accidental explosion. On the left of the passage are two rooms forming the main magazine for the bastion – the first room stored shells, the second stored cartridges. On the rear wall of each room you can see a recess, originally sealed by a glass pane, where a magazine lamp was placed to provide light. There is a ventilator above to keep the room dry and cool. The large stones projecting from the walls of the cartridge magazine held heavy timber racking for stacking the cartridges.

The protective mounds covering the magazines in the north-east bastion

The north-east bastion viewed from its outer tip. The serving rooms and gun emplacements of the 1870s are on the left

Continue along the passage to another, longer passage, leading to four identical storerooms (the exit is to the right).

These storerooms were for a small supply of cartridges and shells, kept separately and ready to supply to the guns above. The two shell stores can be identified by the wooden shelves around the entrance for storing fuses, which were fitted to the shells immediately before use. Each storeroom is positioned directly under a serving room on the rampart above. A circular vertical shaft, going up to the serving room, contained a hoist for hauling up the heavy cartridges and shells. In the end wall is a recessed rectangular shaft, allowing an oil lamp to be lowered from the serving room.

Leave the passage, turn right and go up onto the rampart of the north-east bastion. There are good views of the outer defences here. Continue round to the concrete path and go into the first serving room.

This room received shells from the store below, ready for issue to the gun. In the far right corner, steel doors open onto the shaft down which the lamp was lowered to illuminate the storeroom below. Behind the wooden doors is a ringbolt that once supported the lifting tackle for raising shells from the store; the shaft is now sealed for safety.

Return to the concrete path.

An emplacement for a 10-inch gun in the north-east bastion. Installed in the 1870s, these guns were howitzers (that fired at high angles) to defend the landward side of the fort

This 9-inch RML gun at The Needles Battery on the Isle of Wight is the same as those installed at Tilbury in the 1870s (the emplacement and gun platform are different). When fired, the gun recoiled along the platform for reloading, before being moved forward for another shot

On the right is the earth mound that covers the main magazine. On the left are three identical gun emplacements set between serving rooms. The guns were rifled muzzle-loaders (RML) of 9-inch calibre, each weighing twelve tons and capable of firing a shell 7.25 km (4.5 miles) down river. Each emplacement, sunk to provide protection, contained a gun that fired through the embrasure at the front. The gun sat on an iron platform with small wheels at the front and back, pivoting at the front and turning more at the back, along the curved steel rails visible on the ground. The metal ringbolts in the side walls were for securing the ropes used for lifting tackle when the guns were being installed or removed. The large pipes are a later addition, providing ventilation from the cartridge and shell stores below.

Below: An emplacement for a 9-inch RML gun in the north-east bastion. From the 1870s these guns defended the river as far as the front line fortifications four miles downriver

At the end of the path, go down the ramp, return to the parade ground and turn left to face the officers' quarters.

Officers' Quarters

Officers had better accommodation than ordinary soldiers. This elegant terrace (now partly privately owned) has been rebuilt and altered several times, but the exterior dates from extensive repairs carried out in 1752-3. The small building at the end of the officers' quarters served as a stable.

The interior of the officers' quarters was originally divided into self-contained suites. A junior officer could expect at least two rooms, while high-ranking officers had more. However, in an age when officers bought their positions, many chose to live more comfortably across the river in Gravesend, fulfilling their duties at the fort as required. In 1849, the terrace accommodated seven officers, plus mess and kitchen facilities. Fourteen rooms were allocated to the Ordnance Storekeeper, two rooms served as offices, and eight rooms were for the Commanding Officer.

The Bernard Truss collection of military items and wartime memorabilia is held here. It is a private collection but visitors are welcome to view it.

Pass along the front of the terrace then turn right and go to the far side of the General Artillery Store. Turn to face the rampart.

South-East Curtain

This rampart follows the same pattern as that of the north-east bastion, because it was adapted for the same guns at the same time. The brick serving-rooms are clearly visible. However, further alterations made between 1902 and 1904 created new concrete emplacements by infilling the old open ones. These supported breech-loading guns in the first few years of the 20th century.

Go up the two flights of steps.

The elegant officers' quarters, facing onto the parade ground. They once had small front gardens framed by ornamental railings

Three QF guns on the south-east curtain (from nearest to furthest away): a 6-pdr of 1898, 12-pdr of 1902 and a 12-pdr of 1942

A shell davit for one of Tilbury's 6-inch guns. It is a small crane for lifting shells and other heavy equipment

Opposite: An early 19th-century engraving of the Water Gate by George Cooke, from a drawing by S. Owen

As you go up the second flight of steps, you will notice the strong steel doors over the recesses where ammunition was stored ready for the guns. At the top are four concrete emplacements for 12-pounder quick-firing (QF) guns, for use particularly against torpedo boats. The three guns on display are: a 6-pounder of 1898 (nearest); a 12-pounder of 1902; and a 12-pounder of 1942 (furthest away).

Now turn and walk back past the quick-firing guns and carry on to look at another, very large gun.

As you go, look for two concrete pillars on the left, one rather like a table. This is the gun commander's position, from which the gun crews were controlled. It was originally covered by a flat-roofed timber building with a large observation window at the front.

This large gun is a 6-inch breech-loader, similar to two installed at Tilbury around 1904. It was capable of inflicting serious damage on armoured warships. It has a thick shield to protect its crew and stands in a deep concrete pit, to which cartridges and shells were relayed on lifts from the magazines below. Guns of this calibre were commonly used throughout the British Isles until 1956, when the development of rockets made them obsolete.

Further on is another 6-inch gun emplacement that was modified in the Second World War; it now contains a Blacker Bombard, otherwise known as a spigot mortar. This was a short-range weapon that fired a light projectile against both infantry and tanks. It was commonly used by the Home Guard.

Walk across the back of this last emplacement and go down the steps. Turn left and enter the first doorway.

This is the shell store for one of the 6-inch guns. Against its walls are the steel supports for wooden shelves that supported the heavy 6-inch shells. There is also a well-preserved mechanical lift that was used to transport shells to the emplacement above. The curved steel davit (crane), which you can see on the level above when you leave the building, could also be used for lifting shells and any other heavy equipment up to the gun above.

Cross to the Water Gate.

Water Gate

You will have entered Tilbury Fort through the Water Gate, the fort's impressive monumental entrance. Above the entrance passage, two floors provided accommodation for the master gunner, an important officer in charge of the fort's artillery. To the left of the gate are traces of a building that once stood against the fort wall; this was the sutler's house, occupied by a civilian who sold food, drink and miscellaneous items to the soldiers. In the 19th century it became an official canteen.

Beyond the sutler's house, another entrance to the fort, with large double gates, was broken through the fort wall during the First World War. A few metres further away is the site of the first fort at Tilbury, a blockhouse built in the reign of Henry VIII. Although demolished in the middle of the 19th century, there may be remains of it underground.

As you leave through the Water Gate, have a look at the strong wooden gates ahead of you. The opposite end would have been closed by an identical pair of gates, from which the iron hinge pins survive. The passage enabled security checks to be made on all visitors. Looking back at the Water Gate from the outside, you can see the monumental face, designed to impress and to commemorate the building of the fort in the reign of Charles II. It greeted soldiers and visitors approaching from landing stages on the river and along the road from the ferry a short distance upstream, near what is now The World's End pub. The gatehouse, elaborately faced in carved Portland stone, has an inscription commemorating Charles II (CAROLUS REX). Above it, the empty niche probably held his statue, while at the very top is the royal coat of arms. The intricate carvings of weapons are trophies celebrating the king's achievements in war.

The impressive stone façade of the Water Gate, completed around 1682

HISTORY OF THE FORT

Tudor defence of the River Thames

For centuries, the River Thames was the most important route into England, a vital artery carrying the nation's trade wealth. From the time of the early Tudors there were important arsenals and dockyards at Woolwich and Deptford, where naval vessels were built to protect that wealth. It is not surprising that there is a long history of measures to discourage attack and invasion along the river.

A map of the River Thames showing the position of its blockhouses and forts

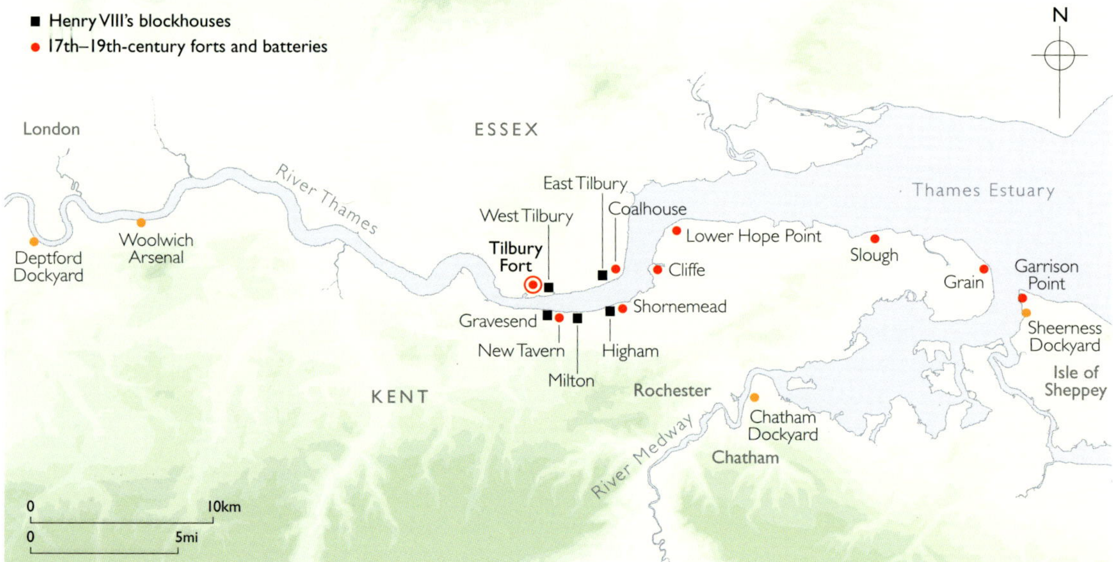

In the 1530s, the policies of Henry VIII led to severe political troubles. Following the Pope's refusal to allow Henry a divorce from Catherine of Aragon, the king had embarked on a process of establishing a Church of England. Henry had discovered that Anne Boleyn was already pregnant and had to marry her to secure the legitimacy of her child, and so could not afford procrastination with the Pope. Early in 1533, an Act in Restraint of Appeals was hurried through parliament, forbidding any appeals to Rome, and later that year there followed an Act of Supremacy, by which Henry established himself as 'Supreme Head of the Church of England'. The breach between the king and the Pope deepened and the Pope responded with excommunication (official exclusion from the Catholic church). In June 1538 a peace treaty was signed between the two rival Catholic powers of Europe – Francis I of France and the Emperor Charles V – raising the prospect of the major powers of Europe uniting in a Catholic crusade against Henry.

In 1539, in response to this threat, Henry began building artillery forts along the east and south coasts of England, in the first national scheme of coastal defence. Five small forts, called 'blockhouses', were established on the Thames at West Tilbury, East Tilbury, Higham, Milton and Gravesend. These were built for artillery to prevent hostile shipping from attacking the river settlements, from proceeding upstream towards London, or from disembarking soldiers. The blockhouses at East Tilbury and Higham formed the front line, establishing a crossfire and also guarding the ferries that were vital for moving troops and supplies to meet enemy landings on both sides of the river. The others – including West Tilbury – formed a second line, guarding another ferry crossing.

Each blockhouse was a squat tower, D-shaped in plan, with thick walls of brick and stone. Artillery was mounted at ground level, in strong enclosed chambers (casemates), and also on the roof, in open positions protected by a parapet. The West Tilbury blockhouse (known initially as 'Thermitage Bullwark' and positioned on the site of the later Tilbury Fort)

Tilbury Fort c.*1799. This view clearly shows the original 1539 blockhouse with a flag flying on its roof*

ELIZABETH AND THE ❖ ARMADA CRISIS OF 1588 ❖

In 1588, following years of simmering conflict between England and Spain, Philip II of Spain sent out a huge fleet to join with an army waiting in the Netherlands under the Duke of Parma, to invade England.

While the English fleet sailed out to fight the Spanish galleons, Elizabeth I ordered emergency repairs to defences and the raising of the 'Citizen Militia'. This makeshift English army gathered around West Tilbury village on a hill overlooking the Thames, waiting for the alarm. On 8th August, Elizabeth met her general, the Earl of Leicester, and the following day, appearing with breastplate and sword, she exhorted the troops at West Tilbury with her famous speech:

'And therefore I am come amongst you at this time, not as for my recreation or sport, but being resolved, in the midst and heat of the battle, to live or die amongst you all; to lay down, for my God, and for my kingdom, and for my people, my honor and my blood, even the dust. I know I have but the body of a weak and feeble woman; but I have the heart and stomach of a king, and of a king of England, too; and think foul scorn that Parma or Spain, or any prince of Europe, should dare to invade the borders of my realms: to which, rather than any dishonour should grow by me, I myself will take up arms.'

Elizabeth I reviewing her army at Tilbury in 1588. This detail of a 17th-century painting from the Church of St Faith, Gaywood (King's Lynn, Norfolk) shows a fanciful representation of the blockhouse on the left

A few days later, news reached Tilbury that the Armada was beaten and in flight; it was unlikely that Parma could embark his invasion force. Although there was great relief that the immediate danger had passed, to be safe, the English army was not disbanded until 17th August, when it was certain that the invasion had failed.

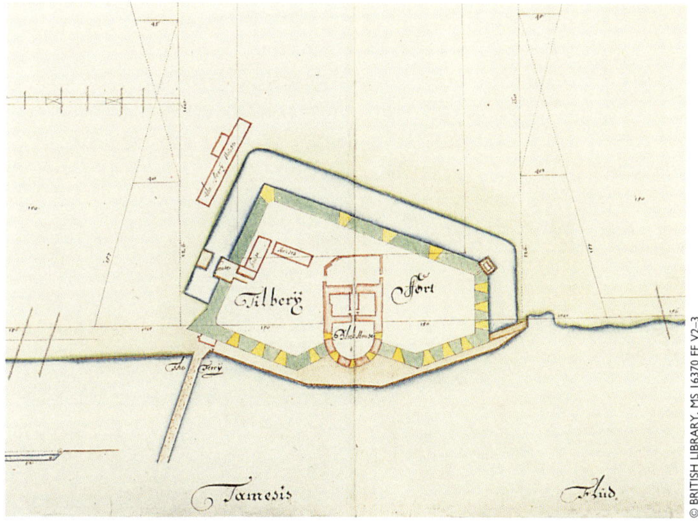

The Tilbury blockhouse, shown on a plan of 1669, but largely as it would have been in the 16th century

stood in a small enclosure, defended by a rampart and ditch. The rampart supported artillery and infantry protecting the blockhouse against assault from the land. The peacetime garrison comprised only nine men: a captain, a deputy, a porter, two soldiers and four gunners, although this complement would have been increased in emergencies.

In 1553, with the Catholic Mary enthroned, the blockhouses were disarmed and, by the time Elizabeth I succeeded to the throne in 1558, most were in bad condition. West Tilbury and Gravesend were repaired but the others were demolished. Emergency alterations at West Tilbury were prompted by the Armada crisis in 1588, and in 1589, when the immediate danger had passed, a larger defended enclosure was made around the blockhouse under the supervision of an Italian engineer, Federico Gianibelli. This enclosed the road to the ferry and enabled defence by a larger force behind two parallel lines of rampart and ditch.

Neglect in the Early 17th Century

Until the 1660s, England had no standing army. Garrison forts were controlled by men of middle rank, who viewed their commands partly as a path to profit and advancement. It was an imperfect system whereby commanders had to petition the government for money to pay their soldiers and keep the forts in good repair. With pay frequently in arrears, garrisons were often smaller than necessary and maintenance was undertaken only when an emergency loomed. Thus Tilbury was allowed to fall into neglect, as highlighted by John Talbot, who complained in 1636 that the outer defences were flooded at high tide, and that ferry passengers and animals regularly intruded.

During the Civil Wars of the mid-17th century, the fort was controlled by the City Militia as a Parliamentary outpost of the defences built around London. In 1649, it became a checkpoint at which ships were required to register the names of their crew and to guarantee their loyalty to Parliament. But its garrison – which in 1651 comprised a governor, two officers, four corporals, a drummer, a master gunner, sixteen gunners and forty-four soldiers – saw no action. Gianibelli's fortified area appears to have been abandoned, leaving the blockhouse inside its original enclosure.

'A Royal work indeede'

Change came about after the Restoration of Charles II in 1660. The new king quickly established a small standing army and permanent garrisons in several strategic locations. At the same time, a review was undertaken of coastal defences, and the Chief Engineer, Sir Bernard de Gomme, began work on improvements.

Sir Bernard de Gomme was born in Turneuzen in the south-western Netherlands in 1620. He came to England in 1641, serving as Engineer and Quartermaster General for Charles I throughout the English Civil War. After the Royalist defeat, he returned to the Continent in 1649, remaining there until the Restoration of Charles II to the English throne in 1660. Charles appointed him Chief Engineer and he served in that capacity until his death in 1685. During that time he designed and managed several large fortification projects, including securing the major naval bases and anchorages at Portsmouth, Plymouth, the Thames, the Medway and Harwich.

Tilbury Fort is probably De Gomme's most accomplished design, and is the most complete example in Britain of a 17th-century bastioned artillery fort with elaborate outer defences. It is modelled on fortifications developed at that time in the Low Countries, where the Dutch were establishing complex defences for their major towns and forts on

Below left: Gianibelli's plan for Tilbury, showing a new rampart and ditch forming a zig-zag defence outside the older blockhouse

Below right: Sir Bernard de Gomme's design for Tilbury, dated 1670. This plan was implemented with the omission of the riverside bastion, while the other four bastions were given just one tier of guns

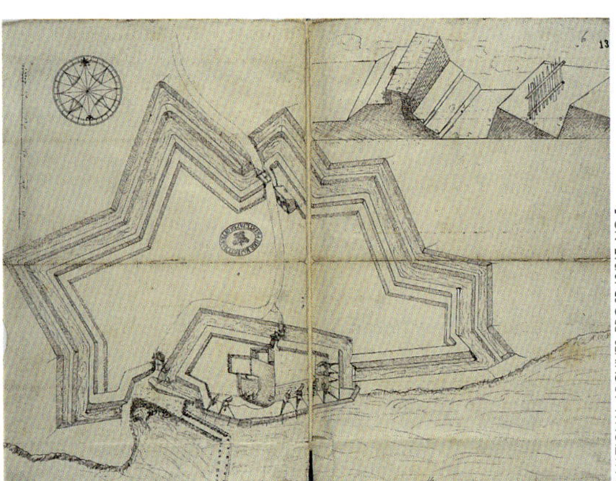

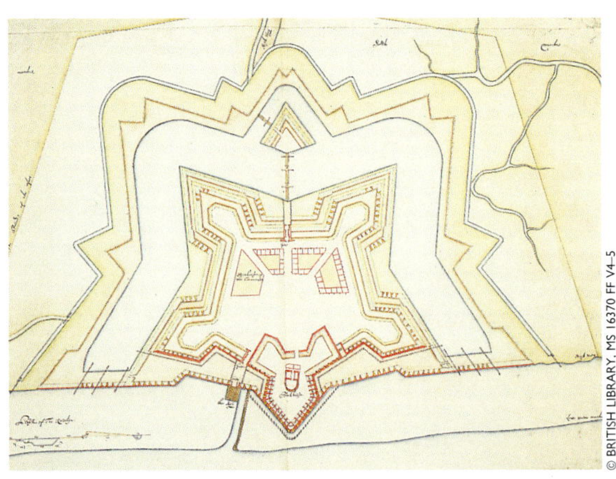

similar wet terrain. Military engineering had become a scientific profession, refined by two contemporaries of De Gomme: Sebastien le Prestre de Vauban and Menno, Baron von Coehorn. These men perfected the bastion system, which had originated in Italy in the early 16th century and which lasted into the early 19th century.

De Gomme drew up designs for a new fort at Tilbury in 1661, but these were never realised. However, revised proposals were put forward in 1667, following a humiliating incident that exposed the inadequacy of the defences on the Rivers Thames and Medway. A Dutch naval squadron sailed unchallenged up the Thames, reaching the Lower Hope, only a few miles from Tilbury. Shortly afterwards, the Dutch fleet entered the Medway, burning part of the English fleet at Chatham and capturing the flagship, the *Royal Charles*. Here at last was the crisis needed for money to be spent on new forts for both rivers. Tilbury was surveyed again in 1667, and by 1670 a design for a new fort was agreed. It is this fort which, to a large extent, survives today.

Portrait of Sir Bernard de Gomme, who designed Tilbury Fort

Building began late in 1670, with up to 265 labourers and craftsmen employed on the works from villages in Essex and Kent, from as far afield as Sittingbourne and Barking, and up to seven officers were engaged overseeing, surveying, storekeeping and accounting. After levelling most of the old fort, the workforce cut new ditches and raised new ramparts – difficult and dirty work on a marshy site. The interior of the fort had to be raised to prevent flooding, while walls and buildings required a solid foundation that was provided by thousands of timber piles, brought by ship from Norway and driven into the marsh.

The construction stretched over fifteen years. Progress was painfully slow and by 1676 the ramparts were only half completed – probably because so many defence projects were being undertaken across the country. To speed work along, several private contractors were engaged, including Sir William Pritchard, a prominent Alderman of the City of London. By 1680 the fort was armed, and by 1685 it was almost finished. Further improvements were made by De Gomme's successor, Sir Martin Beckman, notably the introduction of

❖ TILBURY'S GUNS ❖

Artillery pieces before 1850 are commonly called cannon. Most had smooth-bore barrels and were loaded at the outer 'muzzle' end, with a charge of gunpowder contained in a silk bag. This was ignited to fire a solid shot (such as a cannon ball) or a shell (a hollow sphere containing its own charge that exploded and shattered on its target).

In forts, cannon were mounted on wheeled carriages that recoiled backwards with the impact of firing. For this reason they were placed on sloping platforms so that they could be easily 'run out' to fire again. From around 1800, cannon were placed on traversing platforms, which enabled the gun to be more easily moved and aimed.

In the 1850s, 'rifled' barrels were introduced, which had internal spiral grooves that caused a pointed shell to spin, producing greater speed and accuracy. Both muzzle-loading (RML) and breech-loading (RBL) types were made (the breech is at the rear). The terms 'cartridge' (for the charge) and 'gun' became commonly used.

From the 1880s, breech-loading guns became standard. They were quicker to fire and load, and incorporated 'recoil' mechanisms that ensured they did not leap backwards on firing, and could be moved and aimed around a fixed mounting. Breech-loading guns of up to 10-inch calibre were installed in forts. A group of light, quick-firing (QF) guns could be fired very rapidly, aided by 'fixed ammunition' (where the cartridge and shell were combined into a single unit), and were effective against fast, lightly armoured vessels such as torpedo boats.

Above: a late 18th-century smooth-bored gun at Tilbury, on a wooden truck carriage

Below left: a late 19th-century RML gun at Dartmouth Castle (Devon), mounted on a wooden traversing carriage

Below right: a 6-inch breech-loading gun of about 1900, mounted on a central steel pivot

Tilbury Fort from Gravesend, dated 1773. The union flag is flying from the Tudor blockhouse, while the gun lines can be seen on either side

stone artillery platforms following an inspection of 1694, which showed that many of the wooden ones were already rotten.

By 1700, completed, armed and garrisoned, Tilbury Fort was one of the most powerful fortresses in the land. The main gun batteries – the east and west gun lines – were ranged along the riverbank to protect the passage. However, only four bastions were built out from the main curtain wall; the fifth, intended to project into the river to provide flanking fire along the riverside batteries, was not completed. The old D-shaped tower of the Tudor blockhouse was retained as a gunpowder magazine.

The outer defences, designed to protect the fort from an attack by land, were themselves formidable, comprising two broad moats, filled with water from the Thames, which could be crossed only by timber bridges that incorporated lifting sections. These were guarded by small strong points (redoubts) on triangular islands in the moats. The strip of land between the moats formed an earth rampart, behind which infantry could defend the approaches to the moats, redoubts and bridges. Another small triangular redoubt guarded the approach to the gun lines from the ferry.

GUNPOWDER AND GARRISON IN THE 18TH AND EARLY 19TH CENTURIES

Wars were frequent during this period and, although most were fought at sea, on the Continent or in the colonies, there were several invasion scares. Tilbury Fort was permanently garrisoned, sometimes by regular infantry but increasingly by Invalid Companies of soldiers who were not fit for service on campaign. The artillery was maintained by a caretaker detachment, comprising a master gunner and a few ordinary gunners, that was reinforced in an emergency. In 1715, the gun lines along the riverbank alone contained a formidable battery of seventy-five heavy guns, ensuring Tilbury stood as an effective deterrent against attack.

Early in the 18th century the fort was given an additional role. The government's Board of Ordnance,

❖ A PRISON FOR JACOBITES ❖

The Jacobite rebellion of 1745–6 was the last attempt to restore the Scottish and English thrones to a descendant of James II, who had been deposed in 1688. His grandson, Charles Edward Stuart – known as Bonnie Prince Charlie – led the rebellion which, despite initial successes, ended in defeat at Culloden in 1746. Bonnie Prince Charlie spent months in hiding before leaving Scotland, never to return.

An 18th-century depiction of the Battle of Culloden, 16 April 1746

Of 3500 Jacobite prisoners, 303 sailed from Inverness for Tilbury, enduring appalling conditions of starvation and disease aboard small transport ships. On 11th August 1746, 268 survivors landed and were imprisoned in the powder magazines of Tilbury Fort. Within a month forty-five had died, mainly of typhus. The survivors were tried in London early in 1747. Some were executed, but many were transported to Barbados and Antigua as slave labourers on sugar plantations. Only a few men were released.

A memorial stone to the bravery and suffering of the Jacobite prisoners stands in the lea of the river wall at Tilbury, outside the Water Gate – a sad reminder of cruel times.

which supplied all equipment of war to the Army, used the fort for the storage and supply of gunpowder. Consequently, from around 1716 there were two separate bodies operating at Tilbury: an infantry garrison under the command of a governor (later an army major) and with an artillery detachment seconded to it, and civilian store workers controlled by the Board's storekeeper.

Such was the scale of the Board's operation at Tilbury that a wharf was built on the river solely to shift gunpowder in and out of the fort, and two large powder magazines were constructed on the edge of the parade ground in 1716. Both the old Tudor blockhouse and an ordinary storehouse on the west of the parade ground were converted into magazines, with a cooperage for making barrels. Further storage was provided by De Gomme's original fort magazine in the east bastion. In 1830, the storage capacity at Tilbury exceeded 19,000 barrels of gunpowder, which was a very large quantity.

In 1778, prompted by fear of a major attack on the port of London, Thames defences were again reassessed in a survey by a captain of the Engineers, Thomas Hyde Page. He considered that Tilbury Fort needed a small additional battery of six guns on the outer defences, facing directly downstream. The most significant result of Page's work on the Thames was the building in 1780 of a new fortification, New Tavern Fort, across the river in Gravesend.

During the long years of the Napoleonic Wars (1793–1815) Tilbury Fort continued to fulfil its joint role as garrison and store, but few new works were undertaken. One exception was the re-fitting of the artillery on the gun lines and bastions with traversing platforms to ensure quicker aiming and firing. Repeated invasion scares prompted the building of small batteries downstream at Lower Hope Point, Coalhouse Point and Shornmead, but the major works of the period were concentrated elsewhere, particularly on the new Martello artillery towers on the east and south coasts.

After the end of Britain's hostilities with France, Tilbury continued its duties but spending on defence dried up. Documents suggest a relaxed atmosphere at this time, with vegetable gardens established between the moat and the fort wall, worked by the soldiers to supply themselves and the canteen. Senior officers took the profit of grazing and haymaking from the grass on the parade ground, ramparts and outworks – underlining their continued self-interest. Such financial privileges were standard practice but were extinguished as the century progressed, as military efficiency became paramount.

Coalhouse Fort, built in the 1860s as a new front-line defence for the Thames

A garrison officer of the Royal Artillery in parade order, around 1889

Watercolours of gunners of the Royal Artillery c. *1880. The one on the left is in normal day order (comparing closely with the uniform of the Tilbury gunners on page 7); the one on the right is a gunner equipped for the field*

THE ARMS RACE: REORGANISATION AT TILBURY

In the 1850s there was serious concern in Britain over the build-up of French military and naval resources. An arms race had begun, spearheaded by the first steam-driven ironclad warships – the French *La Gloire* (of 1859), and the British *HMS Warrior* (of 1860). Such vessels had hulls reinforced with thick iron plates against which conventional artillery was ineffective. Steam power allowed these ships to go anywhere in most sea conditions and they carried new artillery with rifled barrels that fired shells with greater accuracy and over longer ranges. In combination with improved explosive warheads, these improvements created an ever more potent threat, and established coastal defences found themselves to be vulnerable.

Against this background, a Royal Commission was appointed in 1859 to review the nation's defences. While the report recognised that the whole country could not be fortified, it resulted in an ambitious ten-year programme to build new forts that would protect the major naval bases, arsenals and the Thames. These new forts were to be constructed on a massive scale, in order to withstand heavy bombardment from rifled artillery, and with a capability to return fire with similar or superior guns.

On the Thames in the early 1860s, new front-line forts were built downstream at Coalhouse Point and Cliffe, while Tilbury found itself in the rear and acting as a second line of defence. Nevertheless, conversion at Tilbury between 1868 and 1871 produced a formidable battery of thirteen new gun emplacements in the west and north-east bastions and along the south-east curtain, mostly facing down the Thames in support of the new forts. Each new emplacement contained a massive rifled muzzle-loading (RML) gun. Most were of 9-inch calibre but one in the east bastion was an 11-inch, weighing 25 tons. New magazines were established in safe, bomb-proof positions under the emplacements, from which ammunition was relayed along tunnels to shell and cartridge stores and up vertical shafts to serving rooms next to each gun. Each emplacement was open to the rear and the sky, but protected on the sides by thick brick walls and earth mounds covering the serving rooms, and in some cases at the front by thick iron shields.

THE LAST GUNS, 1901–3

Such was the pace of technological innovation that, by the start of the 20th century, the RMLs and the forts that held them were soon obsolete. Warships became stronger, faster and more versatile, with powerful and accurate artillery that created an unprecedented threat to highly visible forts on land. The new generation of breech-loading guns could be fired and re-loaded far more quickly than their relatively cumbersome muzzle-loading predecessors. From the late 1880s, these guns were being placed in new batteries built to minimise their visibility, although many were installed in existing forts. Tilbury, at the rear of the Thames defences, had to wait until the start of the 20th century, when four new emplacements were built in concrete on the south-east curtain for quick-firing (QF) artillery. Shortly afterwards two larger 6-inch guns were added. This combination of artillery was designed to prevent small torpedo boats and armoured cruisers from marauding upstream.

The life of these guns was remarkably short. By 1905, it was decided that the Thames was so well defended by the Royal Navy and by breech-loading guns in batteries at the mouth of the Thames and the Medway, that the likelihood of attack this far up the river had become practically non-existent. The guns were still in position in January 1906 but were removed from the fort shortly afterwards, leaving only an infantry garrison equipped with machine guns and small arms for local defence.

Soldiers performing gun drill c. *1884, from the* Illustrated London News

Mobilisation Centre and Ordnance Depot, 1889–1926

While its role in defence of the Thames was in decline, Tilbury Fort continued to store ammunition and other supplies. In 1889, a new scheme was established for defending London in the event of an invasion. The London Defence Scheme was a 72-mile-long theoretical 'stop line' of trenches and strong points. The scheme was not to be put into practice until invasion was imminent, but several mobilisation centres were built beforehand to serve as assembly points and supply bases for a mobile army, where stores could be kept and collected. While most were purpose-built, Tilbury Fort was simply converted. Several large hanger-like buildings of light semi-permanent design were introduced from 1889 to 1890, occupying nearly all of the parade ground, and another was built

Tilbury Fort in 1904; a reconstruction by Frank Gardiner. This shows many buildings that have been demolished, including the mobilisation sheds on the parade ground, the married quarters in the north-west bastion, the canteen next to the Water Gate and a range of service and accommodation buildings next to the soldiers' quarters. By this time the outer defences were not in use

against the outer face of the fort wall between the north-west and west bastions. These structures contained large quantities of waggons and horse harnesses for army transport.

When war broke out in 1914, all the stores at Tilbury were issued and the fort given over to barracks for soldiers destined for France. Over 300 men were accommodated at any one time. Some had to sleep in the magazines, while many more slept in tents in the country nearby. In October 1915, the fort was officially designated as an Ordnance Depot, resuming its supply functions as space was gradually reclaimed from the infantry. By 1917, with only a small infantry guard remaining, the fort was dedicated to the storage and supply of explosives, ammunition, infantry equipment, tents, camp stores, waggons and gun carriages, with a staff of up to seventy-five from the Army Ordnance Department. Electric lighting and motorised transport were introduced, and, during or just after the war, rails were laid for a tramway system to aid movement of supplies.

During these years, the military and commercial installations along the Thames were targets for a new menace: attack from the air. The first air raids by German Zeppelins (airships) and bombers occurred in January 1915. To fight back, anti-aircraft guns with searchlights for night fighting were installed around the district in that year, including one at Tilbury. Known affectionately as 'Screaming Lizzie', it remained at the fort until the end of the war.

The Army Ordnance Department remained at Tilbury after the First World War, when the fort was used as a receiving depot for artillery returning from the war. By 1925, the fort was thought to have outlived its usefulness, although it continued to receive basic care and maintenance. The site was put into the hands of the Commissioners for Crown Lands, who tried, unsuccessfully, to sell it for commercial development. Nevertheless, the old gun lines became a public promenade.

When war broke out again in 1939, the chapel and guard house were converted into an anti-aircraft operations room, controlling and co-ordinating the fire from guns along the river against German bombing raids in the first months of the conflict. The surrounding marshland was criss-crossed by long trenches, designed to prevent enemy troop-carrying aircraft from landing. The anti-aircraft operations room was taken over by a purpose-built control centre at Vange in 1940, after which the fort had no major role in the war, although thousands of troops, tanks and equipment were embarked for D-Day in 1944 from nearby Tilbury Docks.

The Army retained Tilbury until 1950, when the fort was taken into care as a historic monument under the Ministry of Works. A major programme of restoration was undertaken through the 1970s. The fort opened to the public in 1982 and, since 1983, the site has been looked after by English Heritage.

The badge of the Royal Army Ordnance Corps, who served at Tilbury until the 1920s

Further Reading

J. Douet, *British Barracks 1600–1914: Their Architecture and Role in Society*, London, 1998

C. Duffy, *The '45: Bonnie Prince Charlie and the Untold Story of the Jacobite Rising*, London, 2003

N. Hanson, *The Confident Hope of a Miracle: The Real History of the Spanish Armada*, London, 2003

R. Holmes, *Redcoat: The British Soldier in the Age of Horse and Musket*, London, 2002

A. Saunders, *Fortress Britain: Artillery Fortification in the British Isles and Ireland*, Oxford, 1989

A. Saunders, *Fortress Builder: Bernard de Gomme, Charles II's Military Engineer*, Exeter, 2004

V. T. C. Smith, *Defending London's River: The Story of the Thames Forts 1540–1945*, Rochester, 1985

P. M. Wilkinson, 'Excavations at Tilbury Fort, Essex', *Post Medieval Archaeology* **17**, 1983, pp. 111–162

PLAN OF THE OUTWORKS

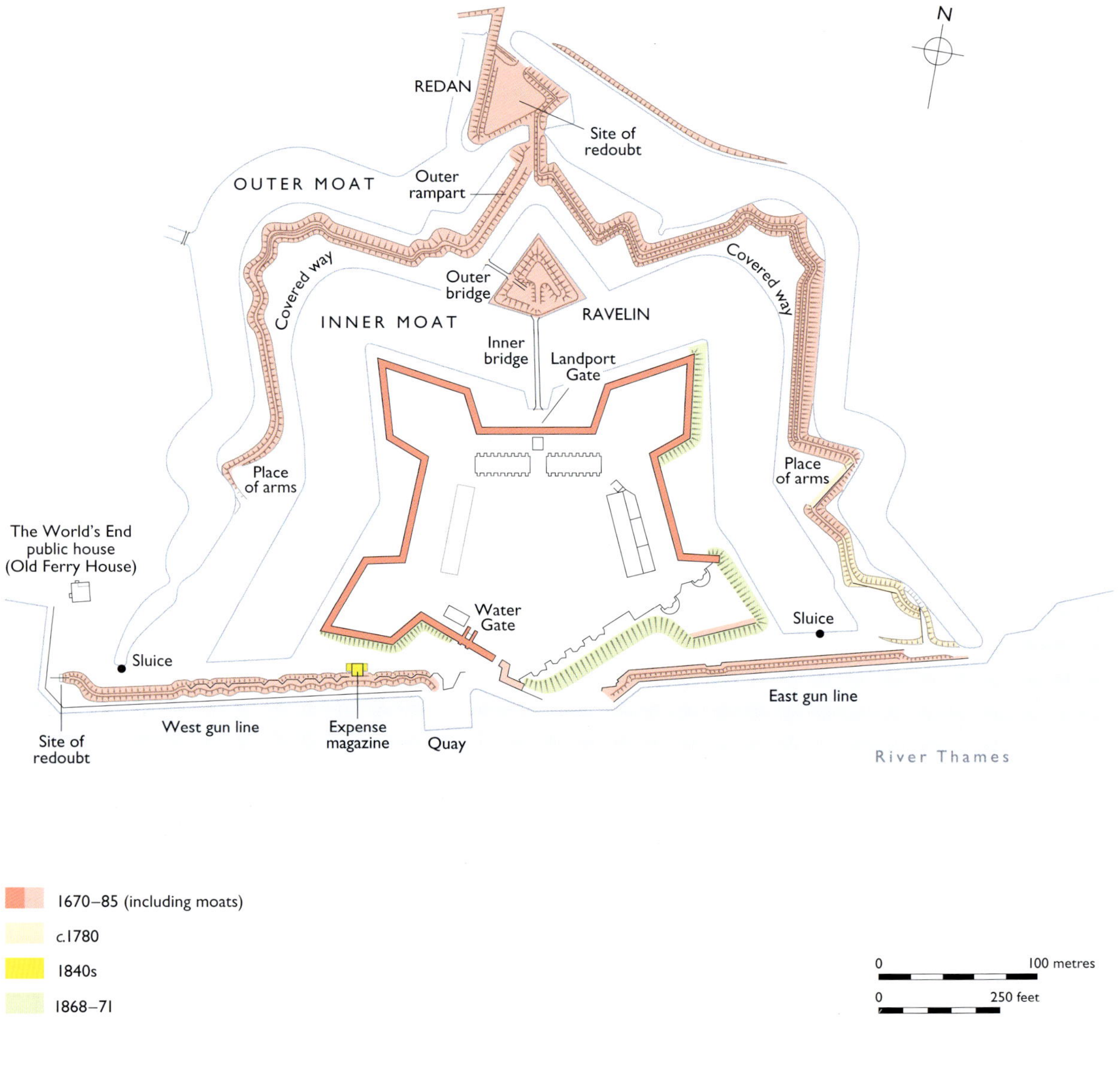
N
REDAN
Site of redoubt
OUTER MOAT
Outer rampart
Covered way
Outer bridge
RAVELIN
INNER MOAT
Covered way
Inner bridge
Landport Gate
Place of arms
Place of arms
The World's End public house (Old Ferry House)
Water Gate
Sluice
Sluice
Site of redoubt
West gun line
Expense magazine
Quay
East gun line
River Thames
1670–85 (including moats)
c.1780
1840s
1868–71
0
100 metres
0
250 feet